cheese

RYLAND
PETERS
& SMALL

LONDON NEW YORK

cheese

discovering, exploring, enjoying

Fiona Beckett
Photography by David Munns

For Jo who loves cheese.

Senior Designer Steve Painter
Editor Miriam Hyslop
Production Patricia Harrington
Art Director Gabriella Le Grazie
Publishing Director Alison Starling

Food Stylist Lucy McKelvie
Stylist Helen Trent
Indexer Hilary Bird

Acknowledgments

Thanks to my two cheese gurus,
Anne-Marie Dyas of the Fine Cheese
Company in Bath and Cheltenham and
Patricia Michelson of La Fromagerie in
London, who have both helped with this
book. Two amazing women. Two wonderful
shops. What they don't know about
cheese isn't worth knowing.

The author and publisher would also like
to thank all at Keen's Dairy and Neal's
Yard Dairy for their help with the book.

First published in the United States
in 2003
by Ryland Peters & Small, Inc.
519 Broadway
5th Floor
New York NY 10012
www.rylandpeters.com

10 9 8 7 6 5 4 3 2

Text © Fiona Beckett 2003
Design and photographs
© Ryland Peters & Small 2003

Library of Congress Cataloging-in-
Publication Data
Beckett, Fiona.
  Cheese : discovering, exploring, enjoying
/ Fiona Beckett ;
photography by David Munns.
      p. cm.
Includes index.
  ISBN-13: 978-1-84172-428-7
  ISBN-10: 1-84172-428-9
  1. Cheese. 2. Cheese--Varieties. 3.
Cookery (Cheese) I. Title.

SF271.B43 2003
641.6'73--dc21
                          2002153694

Notes
Unpasteurized cheese should not be
served to the very young, the very old,
those with compromised immune systems,
or to pregnant women. All spoon
measurements are level unless otherwise
specified. Before baking, weigh or
measure all ingredients exactly and
prepare baking tins or sheets. Ovens
should be preheated to the specified
temperature.

contents

discovering

The moment I discovered that there was more to cheese than a plastic-wrapped slab was when I tasted my first real Cheddar. Several shades deeper than the supermarket version it was dry rather than damp, crumbly rather than smooth, and with a deep rich nutty flavor I had never before encountered. I was hooked.

Since then I've fallen for the charms of goat cheese, at first unfamiliar then so addictive, and for perfectly matured Camemberts and Bries, neither chalky nor running rampant over the cheese board. I've learned to love pungent French washed rind cheeses such as Epoisses, and wondrous alpine cheeses like Beaufort, and even acquired a taste for salty Roquefort. The amazing thing is *not* that much of modern cheese is bland and characterless but just how many cheeses have remained virtually unchanged through the centuries.

The cause of great cheese has also been given a boost by the many passionate individuals who have decided to make their own cheese— some working from old recipes, some inventing new ones, but either way creating modern classics. And to think we can taste them simply by picking up the phone or clicking on a mouse. It has truly never been a better time to be a cheese lover.

why cheese tastes so different

Given that cheese comes from a single ingredient, milk, it's amazing how it can taste—and look—so different. How can the same product be snowy white or deep burnt orange? Be mild enough to eat with fruit or so strong that it overwhelms almost any wine you try to drink with it? Here's how:

the animal the milk comes from

You could in theory make cheese from any milk-producing animal but the three most important sources are cows, sheep, and goats. Cow's milk cheeses are the most popular worldwide, though sheep's cheese is more common in the sparsely vegetated and mountainous areas of southern Europe. Other factors can influence the final cheese, but as a rough generalization cheese made from cow's milk is richer and more creamy, goat cheese more aromatic, and sheep's cheese sharper.

The taste will also depend on the breed of animal, which in some instances is specified by the official rules governing the production of the cheese. For example, Roquefort is produced primarily from the milk of the local Lacaune sheep that graze the Larzac plateau in the Rouergue region of France. There will also be subtle differences depending on the age of the animal and the time of day it is milked.

what the animal feeds on

The dictum "You are what you eat" applies just as much to animals as to humans, and the flavor of cheese can be strongly influenced by whether a herd is out in the open, feeding on lush summer pastures, or eating winter feed. The exact location where the animals graze is important too; the vegetation, the balance of minerals in the soil, the weather, all contribute. For instance, the alpine pastures of the Haute-Savoie with their wild herbs and flowers give a cheese like Beaufort its particularly complex character. Cheese that is made from the milk of animals grazed near the sea may have a more pronounced salty flavor.

the time of year

It's not generally appreciated just how seasonal a product cheese is, how the time of year affects its depth of color as well as its flavor. Young fresh goat's milk cheeses for instance are at their best in spring and early summer. A cheese that needs aging like Stilton may be made from summer milk but will peak in the run up to Christmas. Some cheeses such as Vacherin Mont d'Or (see p.16) are only available at a particular time of year (from September to March). In the spring the same milk is used to make the Gruyère-like Comté.

how the cheese is made

This is the most important factor, particularly in commercially made cheeses. Basically cheese is made by separating out the solid matter of the milk (the curds) from the liquid (the whey) but it may be heat treated, pressed, or molded in various ways (see pp. 12–23). Crucial to the character of the cheese is:

• HOW MUCH FAT IS RETAINED IN THE MILK Parmigiano-Reggiano (Parmesan) for example is made from partially skimmed milk while triple cream cheeses like Explorateur have cream added.

• HOW LONG IT'S MATURED The majority of cheeses will be ready within weeks of being made but some cheeses are matured for very much longer—up to 2–3 years in the case of top quality Parmesan or Gouda. During that time, depending on their style, the cheeses will be regularly turned and their rinds scraped, brushed, or washed.

• THE PRESENCE OF WILD YEASTS AND MOLDS Even under modern hygienic conditions there are natural yeasts and molds in the air of a dairy or maturing room. These can make an apparently identical cheese from one producer taste different from the cheese from another. Nowadays though it is more common for selected molds to be deliberately introduced as they are with blue cheeses (see p. 22).

• WHETHER OR NOT IT IS PASTEURIZED Most milk that is used to make cheese is pasteurized—heat treated to destroy potentially harmful bacteria—but the process can dumb down the flavor too. Most of what are considered the world's greatest cheeses are still made from unpasteurized or raw milk—milk in its natural state. In expert hands it is generally quite safe and gives the cheese its unique personality.

when the cheese is sold

The development of a cheese doesn't end at the dairy. It will carry on evolving when it travels to the distributor and the store where it's finally sold. Admittedly this will be much less marked in the case of factory-made vacuum-packed cheeses than at a specialist shop or restaurant that has a maturing room. Top cheese shops have an expert *affineur* (the French title for someone who matures cheese) who works their own magic on the cheese ensuring that it is sold in the peak of condition. They may even contribute as much to the character of the cheese as the cheesemaker himself.

making traditional cheddar

Cheese consists of only three ingredients—milk, rennet, and salt, and is basically very simple to make.

At Keen's farm in Somerset they have been making Cheddar since 1899. Fresh milk from their own herd is pumped into a large stainless steel vat and heated to 70°F (20°C). A "starter" is added to the vat to sour the milk. Next rennet (an enzyme that alters the protein structure of milk) is added (**1**). This begins to separate the milk, coagulating the richest, solid part (the curds) into a firm jelly-like mass. The resulting gel is cut into very small pieces about the size of a pea, (**2**) to help separate out the

watery residues (the whey). At this stage the curds and whey need to be handled delicately, so as not to loose any more solids.

The mixture continues to be heated up to 105°F (40°C)—the "scald"—in order to expel more liquid. Surprisingly little of the original volume is left after this process—it takes 2½ gallons (10 liters) of milk to make just 2 pounds (1 kg) of cheese.

The mixture is cooled and the soft curds are gently squeezed to extract more of the whey (**3**). The cheese is cut into rough blocks (**4**) which are stacked and re-stacked four times to squeeze out still more moisture (**5** and **6**). The cheese begins to solidify, losing its granular texture, becoming smoother. This process is referred to as cheddaring.

The "bricks" of curd are broken up again and salt is added. This improves the flavor of the cheese and helps to preserve it while it is maturing. The curds are piled by hand into aluminium molds lined with a linen cloth (**7** and **8**) then pressed for 12 hours to extract the last bits of whey (**9**).

Each cheese is dipped in to a hot water bath to help form the rind, then it is wrapped in a plastic cloth, put back in the mold and pressed for a further 24 hours. Once again it is removed from the mold, rubbed with lard and covered with a double layer of muslin (**10**) before going back into the mold for a final 24 hour pressing.

Finally, the 52 lb (26 kg) "truckle" of Cheddar is wrapped in a third layer of muslin. The Cheddar is transferred to a cool aging room where it is left to mature for 12-18 months on wooden shelves (**11**), until its flavor is rich and mellow. The cheese will be regularly turned to ensure it ripens evenly.

soft cheeses

With their mild, sweet flavor soft and semi-soft cheeses
are among the easiest to spread and to eat.

very young cheeses

Cheeses that are days—even hours—rather than weeks old are deliciously light and moussey, the curds just separated from the whey. Goat's and sheep's milk cheeses are often made in this style, and rolled in ash or fresh herbs before serving. Also sold young are fresh, milky **Mozzarella** and its by-product **Ricotta** (see p. 59), which is made from the left-over whey. This style of cheese can be kept longer if preserved in brine or oil, like **Feta** and **Halloumi**. Incidentally, the excess saltiness of Feta can be corrected by soaking it in water or milk for 15 minutes before eating it.

goat cheese

The flavor of goat cheese evolves more rapidly than many other cheeses, so that by the time it is 10 days old the taste may be quite pronounced. Over a few weeks it will develop a natural rind and harden so that the flavor becomes piquant and nutty. Goat's milk cheeses are produced in variety of shapes from small buttons like **Crottin de Chavignol** to logs and pyramids or may be wrapped in vine or chestnut leaves like the Provençal cheese **Banon**.

soft white rind cheeses

Brie and **Camembert** are the two best known examples of this style of cheese which—when young at least—has a delicate mushroomy flavor, creamy texture, and a soft, downy, pure white rind. Most are made from cow's milk. With age they develop in flavor, the center becoming softer and richer until it oozes out of the rind (though this is frowned on by expert *affineurs*). Plenty of artisan producers outside France make cheeses in this style including **Doeling Camembert** from Arkansas and Old Chatham's **Hudson Valley Camembert** from New York. Other examples of soft white rind cheeses are **Chaource**, which comes from the Champagne region of France, the heart–shaped **Coeur de Neufchâtel** from France, and **Cooleeney** from Ireland.

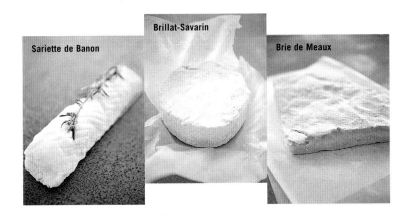

Sariette de Banon

Brillat-Savarin

Brie de Meaux

very creamy cheeses

Made in a similar style to soft rind cheeses but with the addition of cream, which gives them a buttery, unctuous, almost dessert-like richness. They include French cheeses such as **Brillat-Savarin**, **Boursault**, and **Explorateur**.

Taleggio

Epoisses

Pont L'Evêque

gouda-style cheeses

You could argue about how best to describe waxy cheeses like **Gouda**. Technically they're classified semi-soft, though aged Gouda has all the firmness, bite, and richness of flavor of a hard cheese. However if it comes from a supermarket it's more than likely to be mild to mellow in flavor and more soft than hard. Other examples would be **Edam**, **Colby**, and young British and Irish gouda-style cheeses such as **Coolea** and **Teifi**.

semi-soft cheeses (medium-matured)

A description that covers a multitude of unpressed cheeses which share a supple springy consistency and a soft pliable, sometimes sticky rind. Many are categorized as "washed rind". This means the cheese has been washed or rubbed in brine, wine, or cider, giving the cheese a rich fruity flavor and the rind a deep orange color. France has been the master of this style of cheese since the days it was made in the monasteries; in fact it's often referred to as Trappist cheese. Young—or commercially produced—washed rind cheeses such as **Pont L'Evêque**, **Reblochon**, and **Saint-Nectaire** are comparatively mild. But along with others such as **Livarot** and **Maroilles** they can develop pungent flavors and strong, barnyardy aromas that are challenging to all but the cheese aficionado (see Strong Cheeses p. 24). Irish cheesemakers also make some fine washed rind cheeses including **Adrahan**, **Gubbeen**, and **Milleens** that are on the milder side of the spectrum. **Taleggio** is a great Italian example. Good starting points for exploring this style of cheese are the less assertive **Chaumes**, **Morbier**, and **Port-Salut** from France, Danish **Havarti**, and German **Tilsiter**.

vacherin

So special is **Vacherin** that France and Switzerland, which both border the area where it's made, have battled over the name for years. The Swiss finally conceded the French version could be referred to as **Mont d'Or**. Made from unpasteurized milk from cows that graze in the Jura mountains, it has the most fabulous rich, mellow taste and velvety texture. Only available from September to March, it's always presented in a lidded wooden box and when fully ripe you can literally spoon out the contents.

Saint-Nectaire

hard cheeses

The word "hard" applies to cheeses with a firm texture which have been pressed or subjected to heat. They are generally aged and have a hard, inedible rind, though some like Caerphilly or Lancashire can be mild and crumbly.

traditional regional cheeses

A range of historic "territorial cheeses" from different parts of England, some of which date back to the 11th century. Some are mild, creamy, and crumbly like **Caerphilly**, **Wensleydale**, and **Cheshire** (which was mentioned in the Domesday book of 1056). **Lancashire** can have more bite, while **Red Leicester**, and **Double Gloucester**, which owe their orange color to the natural coloring annatto, are richer and nuttier. It's always worth seeking out matured farmhouse versions of these cheeses as mass-produced ones can be bland.

Wensleydale

Montgomery's Cheddar

Keen's Cheddar

Berkswell

Pecorino

cheddar

The most popular style of cheese worldwide, though true Cheddar is only made in the counties of Somerset, Dorset, and Devon, in the south-west of England. The flavor can range from mild and mellow to nutty and piquant depending on whether it is commercially made or aged for months by a farmhouse producer. The average aging would be about 4 months, though artisanal cheddars might well be aged for up to 24 months or even longer. The cheeses are produced in huge dramatic looking "truckles" weighing 52 lb (26 kg) or more and are traditionally wrapped in cheesecloth and sealed with wax. Almost all Cheddars and cheddar-style cheeses are made with cow's milk. Highly regarded English producers include **Montgomery** and **Keen's**. Scotland, Australia, Canada, and New Zealand also have a long history of making good quality cheddar-style cheeses and there are some good artisanal examples in the US such as **Grafton Village Cheddar**. If you like Cheddar you'll also like French **Cantal**.

hard sheep's cheese

Often the product of inhospitable pastures and subsistence farming, sheep's milk cheeses provided vital sustenance for poorer communities across southern Europe and were made to last through the winter. Today such cheeses as Italian **Pecorino** (and its regional variations **Pecorino Romano**, **Pecorino Sardo**, and **Pecorino Toscano**), Spanish **Manchego**, **Roncal**, and **Zamorano**, and **Etorki** and **Ossau-Iraty-Brébis** from the French side of the Pyrénées, are highly regarded for their complexity and depth of flavor. A new generation of cheesemakers in the UK and the US has also chosen to work with sheep's milk rather than cow's milk, creating modern classics such as **Berkswell**, **Spenwood**, and **Vermont Shepherd**. When young this style of cheese has a subtle salty, nutty tang.

swiss-style

Although thought of as Swiss, cheeses such as **Gruyère** and **Emmental** are also made in France; they share the same firm, smooth, close texture which derives from heating the curds then pressing them heavily. The distinctive holes in Emmental and similar cheeses come from bubbles of gas that develop during the fermentation process. The taste is fresh and aromatic, becoming nuttier with age. They also melt well, so are often used in cooking (see p. 54). Traditionally they are made from unpasteurized cow's milk from alpine herds. Less well-known cheeses that are made in a similar way include **Beaufort** and **Comté** from the French side of the Alps, Swiss **Appenzeller** and **Tête de Moine**, and Norwegian **Jarlsberg**. Interesting newer cheeses made in this style include **Gabriel** from Co. Cork in Ireland, **Roth Kase Gruyere** from the US, and **Heidi Gruyere** from Tasmania.

provolone

Scalded and then molded into a myriad of different shapes, this buttercup yellow '*pasta filata*' (stretched curd) cheese is a staple of Italian delis. It can be mild (*dolce*) or aged for up to 2 years (*piccante*).

dutch-style

While much of the **Gouda** you come across is quite soft in texture, mature Gouda is a hard, slightly granular cheese with a rich, nutty flavor much admired by other cheesemakers, who have copied it all over the world. Examples are **Coolea** from West Cork in Ireland, **Teifi** from Wales, **Mahoe Aged Gouda** and **Meyer Vintage Gouda** from New Zealand, and **Bulk Farm Gouda** from California. Deep orange French **Mimolette**, which is made just over the border from Holland, is one of the best cheeses to serve with red Bordeaux.

Parmigiano-Reggiano

grating cheeses

The king of grating cheeses is undoubtedly Parmesan though the term tends to be used of any cheese made in a similar crystalline, crumbly style. True Parmesan is labelled as **Parmigiano-Reggiano** and comes from the Emilia-Romagna region of Italy around the cities of Parma and Modena, where it is aged for up to 4 years (1–2 years is more common). **Grana Padano**, which looks very similar, is usually younger and can come from anywhere in Italy. Other cheeses that grate well include **Pecorino Romano** (see p. 19), **Ricotta Salata**, Swiss **Sbrinz**, and **Vella Dry Jack** from California.

Gouda Boerenkaas

blue cheeses

Among the most colorful additions to a cheese board, blue cheeses are quite distinctive in their appeal. Harmless molds, introduced into the cheese at regular intervals, allow the characteristic greenish-blue "veins" to develop, creating assertive flavors.

mature, mellow blues

Mature blues combine a sharp, assertive flavor with a rich creamy texture which comes from several weeks maturing. Most are made from pasteurized or unpasteurized cow's milk and have a rough, crumbly grayish or orangey crust. They include top English and Irish blues such as **Stilton** (opposite), **Blue Vinny**, **Shropshire Blue**, and **Cashel Blue** as well as French blues such as **Bleu d'Auvergne**, **Bleu de Gex**, and **Fourme d'Ambert**, a fine traditional cheese from the mountainous Auvergne region. America's **Jersey Blue** and **Great Hill Blue** and Australia's award-winning **Gippsland Blue** are other examples.

mild creamy blues

Soft white rinded brie-style cheeses can be made in a blue version—such as **Bresse Bleu** and **Cambozola**, a modern cross between **Camembert** and **Gorgonzola**. Mild (*dolce*) Gorgonzola (see opposite) or **Dolcellate**, as it is sometimes known, also falls into this category—a good starting point for those new to blue.

strong, tangy blues

These are blues with a real bite. **Roquefort** (see opposite) is the best known but other sheep's milk cheeses such as **Beenleigh Blue** from Devon, Scottish **Lanark Blue**, and Spanish blues such as **Cabrales** and **Valdeon** pack a similar punch. Less costly is **Danish Blue**, an inexpensive commercial blue with a powerful flavor that works best in salads and blue cheese dressings.

Cabrales

Fourme d'Ambert

the world's best blues

Stilton

Arguably the greatest English cheese, production of which is only allowed in a very limited area of Derbyshire, Leicestershire, and Nottinghamshire, in the heartland of the country. Made from cow's milk and characterized by its creamy texture, mature mellow flavor and distinctive rough, crumbly grayish rind, it's the traditional cheese to serve at Christmas. Colston Bassett is the most famous producer.

Gorgonzola

Rich, lush Gorgonzola, made using cow's milk, comes from Lombardy and Piedmont in the north-west of Italy. It can be comparatively mild (*dolce*) or strong (*naturale* or *piccante*) and is always sold wrapped in foil which helps preserve its creamy texture. Gorgonzola also lends itself well to cooking.

Roquefort

The strongest and saltiest of blue cheeses, Roquefort is the espresso coffee of the cheese world—a real artisanal unpasteurized sheep's cheese that requires time to fully appreciate. Roquefort is still made in caves in Combalou in the south-west of France where it has been produced since Roman times. The French venerate it like foie gras and truffles, often serving it with the fine dessert wine Sauternes.

strong cheeses

Not everyone likes strong, pungent cheeses but aficionados adore them.
Although the description covers a range of styles the majority come
from the semi-soft washed rind style, the classic French "smelly cheese".
If kept in perfect condition they can be magnificent but should be put
on a cheese board with caution as they can make wine matching tricky.

Adrahan

the stinkers

You can find milder versions of these cheeses but if you spot the following on a cheese counter or trolley expect them to pack quite a punch: **L'Ami du Chambertin**, **Epoisses**, **Livarot**, **Maroilles**, and **Munster** from France and **Limburger** from Germany.

Maroilles

powerful blues

Strong and salty cheeses such as **Roquefort** and Spanish **Cabrales** can overwhelm other cheeses on a cheese board.

unusual flavors

Expect the unexpected. Cheeses that don't taste like any others you've tasted before include the deep caramel-colored almost sweet **Gjetost**, a hugely popular cheese from Norway, and Hungarian **Liptauer**, an intensely spicy soft cheese seasoned with garlic, capers, anchovies, and paprika.

flavored cheeses

Cheese can be flavored with any number of ingredients from apricots to Worcestershire sauce and chutney. Most tend to be made by large commercial companies, though herbs, garlic, and spices are all used by artisanal producers either to flavor the cheese or to replace the rind. The most successful are:

Caprini Tartufo

• HERBS Popular—along with garlic—in soft French cheeses such as **Boursin** and **Le Roulé** and for flavoring the exterior of goat's milk cheeses such as **Chèvrefeuille** and the Corsican **Fleur du Maquis**. They are also used in some traditional English hard cheeses such as **Sage Derby** and **Double Gloucester**.

• GARLIC AND PEPPERCORNS The two key ingredients in one of the best flavored cheeses, **Gaperon**, a white rinded French cheese from the Auvergne.

• CUMIN AND CARAWAY SEEDS Simple but effective additions to fine Dutch cheeses such as **Leiden** and **Gouda**.

• TRUFFLES A glorious addition to cheese—as they are to anything else. The Italians do it best. Look out for the **Caprini Tartufo** from Piedmont.

• SMOKED CHEESES If you like other smoked foods you'll enjoy smoked cheeses, though not everyone feels the natural flavor of a good cheese should be masked by bonfire aromas. Smoked **Mozzarella**, or **Scamorza**, is worth trying.

exploring

There's nothing as thrilling as that faint, clean smell of cheese as you walk into a real cheese shop. The riot of colors as you look around you—pale yellow, rich gold, deep orange, jagged streaks of blue. The glistening olives and the basket of freshly baked crusty bread—there's always bread. But above all the opportunity to nibble and taste and talk. Use a visit to find out as much as possible about different cheeses—how to store them so that you too enjoy them in the peak of condition, and how to serve them so that they look—and taste—their very best. Here's some pointers to get you going.

buying cheese

Given that cheese is one of the few products you can taste before buying, it makes sense to buy it from a specialty cheese shop or the cheese department of large gourmet grocery stores that will readily offer you samples to try. Good cheese shops have knowledgeable and enthusiastic staff who can tell you which cheeses are at their best and in season, how they're made, where they come from, and how best to combine them on a cheese board. That's not to say that an independent shop is automatically better than a supermarket. Some make the mistake of having too big a selection so that the turnover is slow and the cheeses remain too long on the counter. The very best shops actually mature the cheeses "in-house" so they are sold in the peak of condition.

If you buy from a cheese shop regularly they'll become aware of your preferences and should instantly be able to suggest cheeses that you will enjoy. Many also operate a mail-order or internet-based delivery service so you can order cheese from a good shop even if you don't live in the area. But don't ever pass up the opportunity to go and taste in person. It's the best way to find out about cheese!

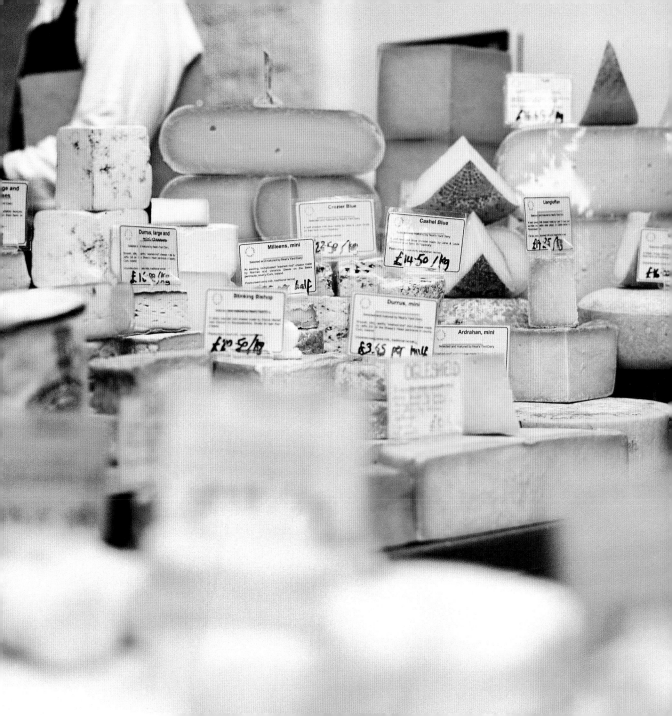

farmer's markets

With cheese, as with every other kind of product, a farmer's market gives you the opportunity to buy from the producer direct. You'll never have the choice that you get in a store or a supermarket but there's a great deal of pleasure in getting to know a producer well and tracking how their cheese changes through the seasons. Very often it's the simplest cheeses that are best bought this way—young goat cheese just a couple of days old can be truly delicious.

supermarkets

It's hard to fault supermarkets on their range of cheeses these days. Even though some cheeses can be very bland, others can be as good as you'd find in a specialty shop. The downside is that you can't taste before you buy so you have to make your own judgement as to whether a cheese is ready to eat. With softer cheeses like Brie and Camembert the best way is to press the center of the cheese gently with the ball of your thumb. It should be beginning to soften.

how much cheese to buy?

Obviously it depends how much cheese you eat, but it's better to buy no more than you are likely to consume over the next couple of days. Treat cheese like other fresh produce such as meat, fish, fruit, and vegetables, rather than something that can be stored for a long time (see also p. 32).

storing

The two main enemies of cheese are excessive heat and air. Heat makes it deteriorate rapidly. Leaving it open to air will dry it out and leave it prey to the bacteria that cause mold. The ideal conditions are those found in a good cheese shop—cool and slightly humid, but few of us have a larder or cellar these days. That leaves the refrigerator as the only realistic possibility; but preferably in a warmer part. Check the manufacturer's instruction manual for advice.

You need to wrap the cheese properly. The original wrapping—whether it's a tub, a wooden box, or waxed paper is the best option but if you open a cheese that's been vacuum packed or have to re-wrap a cheese, waxed or parchment paper or aluminium foil is generally better than plastic wrap which can make the cheese moist and sweaty. However, plastic wrap is an acceptable way of wrapping blue cheeses and hard grating cheeses like Parmesan. Beware of putting cheeses together in a plastic container as milder cheeses may pick up flavors from stronger ones.

It's advisable not to keep cheeses too long once you cut into them. Softer cheeses and cheeses that have already been matured by a cheese shop will deteriorate quicker than harder ones and should ideally be consumed within 1–2 days. If you keep them for longer, re-wrap them regularly.

Can you freeze cheese? Purists would say no, but if you have more cheese left over than you are able to eat immediately it makes sense, though be prepared for a loss of quality. Hard cheeses generally freeze better than softer ones. Grating them first makes them easier to use.

serving rules

The most important thing is to take your cheese out of the refrigerator at least an hour ahead of serving. You only get the full flavor at room temperature. You should also wait to cut it up until just before serving. The moment it's cut cheese begins to dry out.

Ideally you should have a different knife for each type of cheese so that you don't smear soft cheeses on hard ones or mingle strong cheeses with mild ones. For a more informal occasion, like a picnic, use a napkin to wipe the knife before cutting each cheese. You can buy special cheese knives with holes in them that make it easier to cut through softer cheeses such as Camembert or Pont l'Evêque. Cheese slicers are useful when you need fine slices for sandwiches.

When you cut from a cheese that's already been cut in a wedge, try and cut a long thin slice rather than simply cut off the tip. Smaller circular cheeses can be cut into wedges, while harder cheeses like Pecorino taste better cut into fine slices rather than chunks or cubes. Cheeses like Parmesan should always be grated or served in small chunks broken off from the block.

Don't remove the rind beforehand, even though you may not want to eat it. It's a question of taste rather than safety, though most people would be inclined to discard harder rinds or the rinds of pungent cheeses which can be stronger than the cheese itself. Obviously don't eat a waxed rind.

A classic French Abbaye cheese, unsalted butter, and cider jelly

enjoying

Cheese is an opportunity to be creative. To mingle different colors, shapes, and flavors. To compare and contrast different textures and tastes. Sure, there are some classic combinations that it's hard to improve on—cheeses that are natural bedfellows, partnerships of cheese and other ingredients such as the classic Mozzarella, tomato, and basil, sublime cheese and wine matches such as goat cheese and Sauvignon Blanc. But there are others out there waiting to be discovered. The best cheese course I had recently was at a simple bistro in Paris. The chef came from Brittany and served a single traditional cheese from his region—an Abbaye de Timadeuc. He placed it on a rugged slate and accompanied it with a little pot of unsalted farmhouse butter, some delicious cider jelly, and some crusty country bread—sheer magic. Change the way you think about cheese. Be bold.

cheese boards

If you're serving cheese to guests you'll generally want to offer some choice. Not everyone likes—or can eat—the same kind of cheese. Some are intolerant of cow's milk for instance. Others can't stand strong blues. Ardent cheese lovers really appreciate the interplay of colors, shapes, and flavors you get with a selection of different cheeses.

While you can theme a cheese board—all Italian cheeses, say, or all goat's milk cheeses—most people tend to opt for a board that reflects cheeses of different origin, flavor, and texture. You will probably want to include (though there may be some overlap between these categories):

• A sheep's and/or a goat cheese as well as cow's milk cheeses.
• Cheeses from more than one country.
• A range of textures—from soft and creamy to hard.
• A range of flavors—from mild to strong.
• A range of colors. It would be normal to include at least one blue. Orange washed rind cheeses always look colorful too.
• A range of shapes and sizes from circular cheeses to wedges.

For example, your cheese board might feature a local young goat cheese you'd bought from the farmer's market, a small washed rind cheese such as Saint Marcellin, a wedge of mature Cheddar, and a blue sheep's milk cheese. Or if you wanted to compare and contrast different cheeses you could pick three cheeses of the same type— say, three sheep's milk cheeses, or three different blues.

Clockwise from back: Harbourne Blue, Montgomery's Cheddar, Explorateur, Sariette de Banon, Saint Félicien

presenting the cheese

Conventionally cheeses tend to be arranged on a wooden board or marble slab but slate can also look very attractive. A shallow wicker basket will look appealingly rustic, particularly if it's lined with vine leaves, but in general it's better for the surface to be flat rather than hollowed (which makes cutting the cheeses difficult). An alternative presentation would be to plate the cheeses for each person as they do in restaurants. The conventional way to arrange them would be to progress clockwise from soft to hard and mild to strong, but you could break from that by presenting the cheese with different accompaniments. Ones that go well with a range of cheeses include grapes, dried moscatel raisins, fresh medjool dates, quince paste (*membrillo*), walnuts, and pecans. You'll also want some kind of bread or crackers (see pp. 44–49).

how much to serve?

It depends what role the cheese board plays in the meal. If it's the main course following on from, say, a soup or a salad or the focus of a party allow for about 6 oz per person in total. If you are offering some cheese before a meal or after dessert, your guests probably won't want more than 3 oz.

ordering cheese in a restaurant

What should be a pleasure for cheese lovers can sometimes seem more like a test as the waiter stands expectantly waiting for you to select from the 30-odd cheeses on offer. In fact he (or she) will probably be delighted if you give him the chance to show off his expertise. Although you may want to avoid certain styles of cheeses you know from past experience you haven't enjoyed, regard it as an opportunity to experiment.

Clockwise from back: Pecorino Sardo, Gorgonzola Cremificato, Taleggio Valsassina, Caprini Tartufo

Simply irresistible …
Brie and **cherries**. That simple. That good.

cheese plates

The cheese plate is for the cheese lover who likes to partner
a cheese with a perfect accompaniment. They've become a
fashionable way to round off a meal but can equally well be
served as a light lunch, for supper, or a quick snack.

Summer perfection ...
Fresh moussey **goat cheese** with a delicate **herb salad**—
include chervil, flat leaf parsley, chives, and maybe a few
edible flowers. Season lightly with freshly ground black
pepper, sea salt, and a mild olive oil.

Traditional ploughman's lunch ...
Real **farmhouse Cheddar**, home-made **chutney**, a good
apple, and some home-baked **crusty bread**.

Classic but unbeatable ...
Slices of milky **Mozzarella di Bufala**, ripe **tomatoes**, and torn
basil, drizzled with olive oil, and seasoned with black pepper.

Tapas-style ...
Nibble some Spanish **Manchego** cheese with a few slices of
Serrano ham, fat **green olives**, and **roasted almonds**.

Italian sophistication ...
Thin shavings of **Parmesan**—amazing with raw vegetables
such as **fresh fava beans** in the spring or very fine slices
of raw **fennel** dressed with olive oil.

Beautiful colors, fabulous flavors ...
Chunks of **watermelon** and **Feta**, drizzled with extra virgin
olive oil. Grind over a little black pepper and sprinkle a few
pumpkin seeds or black olives round the plate.

to round off a meal

Cheese can be served French-style in between a main course and dessert or in lieu of dessert all together. Fruit—fresh or dried—is fabulous with cheese, particularly apples and pears. So—more surprisingly—is honey (see also Sweet Cheese p. 58).

Summer treat ...
Fresh figs and **Gorgonzola**. Simply made for each other but you do need perfectly ripe juicy figs and a perfectly matured, not overripe cheese.

Pungent and palate-provoking ...
A classic combination from Alsace. **Munster** with **caraway seeds** can be strangely addictive.

A great winter plate ...
Cashel Blue with **chestnut honey** and **roasted chestnuts**.

Stellar match ...
Pear, **Stilton**, and **walnuts**. The walnuts should be freshly shelled or toasted. The pears could also be poached in red wine.

Daringly different ...
A fruity **French "Abbaye" cheese** with unsalted **Normandy butter** and **cider jelly**.

Spain on a plate ...
Manchego with **membrillo**. The country's best known sheep's cheese with its delectable quince paste.

bread and biscuits

bread

Bread is as essential to the enjoyment of cheese as cream is to strawberries or bacon to eggs. There's really nothing like a good hunk of Cheddar and a freshly baked loaf of bread—true food of the gods. Good all-rounders are sourdough and other rough country breads, crusty whites, ciabatta, and flatbreads. What you need is some texture to set against the smoothness and richness of your cheese. Breads that generally work less well are soft milk breads and other sweet breads and those that are already flavored with cheese—too much of a good thing. Some breads seem tailor-made for certain cheeses.

perfect partners

- **French baguette** and **Brie**.
- **Walnut bread** with **blue cheese**.
- **Olive bread** with **goat cheese** or **Feta**.
- **Irish soda bread** with **Durrus**.
- **Pumpernickel bread** with **Cheddar**.
- **Light rye** with **Emmental**.

biscuits

Biscuits are more controversial. Some experts say they detract from the cheese but personally I like them, providing they're not too sweet. Crackers and water-biscuits are probably the most flexible and oatcakes work well with English regional cheeses and the creamy oatmeal-coated Scottish cheese Caboc. Flavored biscuits can be quite effective—for color as well as taste. Caraway and fennel seeds balance the pungency of strong cheeses such as Munster while biscuits flavored with herbs have an affinity with lighter creamier cheeses like young goat cheese. Charcoal biscuits can look fabulous with a snowy white cheese.

should you serve butter?

It's a question of taste and the type of cheese. With hard British cheeses like Cheddar, a good unsalted farmhouse butter is often quite welcome, though it really isn't necessary with a soft creamy cheese like Explorateur. No-one's telling you you can't though.

raisin and rosemary bread

A quick, simple bread that's perfect for cheese. This bread goes well with all kinds of cheeses especially young goat's milk cheeses, cheddar-style cheeses, and creamy blues.

8 oz all-purpose flour and a little extra for dusting

5 oz whole wheat flour

3½ oz rye flour

1½ teaspoons quick-acting yeast

1½ teaspoons fine sea salt

1 tablespoon finely chopped fresh rosemary leaves plus 2 extra sprigs for topping

1½ cups water (tepid if you're making it by hand, cold if you're using a machine)

1 tablespoon soft dark brown sugar

2 tablespoon olive oil

3½ oz raisins

Makes one medium-size loaf

In a bread machine:

Add the liquid and solid ingredients in the order recommended in your manual, leaving out the raisins. Set to knead on the dough program, adding the raisins at the beep. Shape and cook.

Mix together the all-purpose, whole wheat, and rye flours in a large bowl. Mix in the yeast, sea salt, and rosemary. Dissolve the sugar in 2 tablespoons of the water. Make a well in the middle of the flour and pour in the dissolved sugar and olive oil, followed by the rest of the water. Start working the flour into the liquid with a wooden spoon then mix with your hands until all the flour is incorporated.

Turn the dough onto a floured board or work surface and knead for 5 minutes or until the dough begins to feel elastic. Flatten the dough and add half the raisins. Fold over and knead for a couple of seconds then repeat with the remaining raisins. Carry on kneading for another 5 minutes until smooth. Place the dough in a large bowl covered with a lightly dampened dish towel and leave for about 45–50 minutes until doubled in size.

Tip the dough out of the bowl and press down on it to knock out the air. Roll up the dough into a long sausage shape, tucking in the ends. Place on a lightly oiled baking sheet, make 3–4 diagonal cuts in the dough with a sharp knife, cover with the towel, and leave for another 25 minutes.

Preheat the oven to 400°F. Brush the top of the loaf lightly with water and scatter over the remaining rosemary leaves, pressing them lightly into the dough.

Bake for about 35–40 minutes until the loaf is well browned and sounds hollow when you tap it on the base.

Cool on a wire rack for a good 45 minutes before serving.

There's absolutely no point in baking biscuits yourself if nobody knows they're homemade, and the distinctive shape of these very easy crackers makes it clear they're not store bought. They're versatile enough to accompany most cheeses.

garlic and poppyseed
cream crackers

8 oz all-purpose flour, and a little extra for dusting

1 teaspoon baking powder

½ teaspoon fine sea salt

1 teaspoon poppy seeds

4 tablespoons unsalted chilled butter

⅓ cup light cream

½ teaspoon finely chopped garlic

3 tablespoons water

two lightly greased baking sheets

Makes 14–18 large crackers

Preheat the oven to 375°F.

Sift the flour, baking powder, and salt into a large bowl. Add the poppy seeds. Cut the butter into cubes and rub into the flour. Mix the cream with the garlic and stir into the flour then gradually add the water, pulling the mixture together until it forms a ball. (This can also be done in a food processor.)

Flour your work surface or a board and shape the dough into a flat smooth disc. Cut it in half and roll out each half thinly and evenly. Using a sharp knife cut the dough into long triangles, about 6 in. long. Transfer them with a spatula to a baking sheet and prick them all over. Repeat with the remaining dough then roll any trimmings together and re-roll to make a final batch of crackers.

Bake in the oven for about 15 minutes or until lightly browned then set aside on a rack to cool.

Variations:

Cumin and turmeric crackers Sift ½ teaspoon turmeric with the flour. Replace the poppyseeds with 1 teaspoon of cumin seeds. Leave out the garlic. Good with soft goat's and sheep's milk cheeses.

Fennel crackers Replace 3 oz. of the flour with whole wheat flour. Leave out the garlic and replace the poppyseeds with 1½ teaspoons fennel seeds. Lovely with washed rind cheeses such as Munster and Reblochon.

Paprika and chile crackers Sift ½ teaspoon of paprika with the flour. Replace the poppyseeds with several turns of a chile-based spice grind. Delicious with rich creamy cheeses.

Rioja and
Montgomery's Cheddar

cheese and wine

A chunk of cheese, a hunk of freshly baked crusty bread, a glass of wine—the perfect pre-dinner snack.

So why is drinking your favorite wine with cheese so often a disappointment? The usual answer is that we're too ambitious, laying on too many different styles of cheese to give the wine a chance, and that we tend to head for red wines when white or even a glass of sweet wine would be a better match. If you do want to drink red with a variety of different cheeses the best wines to choose are aged Spanish reds like Rioja, mature Italian reds such as Amarone, or older vintages of New World Cabernet Sauvignon and Shiraz that are not too oaky. Or for a less formal occasion a simple fruity wine like a Côtes-du-Rhône. Young tannic reds such as Cabernet and Chianti are the ones that are most likely to clash. Even then it's worth avoiding cheeses that are bound to cause problems like very strong, salty blues, or pungent washed rind cheeses such as Epoisses or Maroilles. Artisanal cheeses are more demanding than commercially produced cheeses but, if you find the right match, more rewarding. If it's the wine you want to show off choose a single fine cheese that will complement it. Wines and cheeses from the same area tend to go well. For example Sancerre and Crottin de Chavignol, both from the Loire, and Gewurztraminer and Munster from Alsace.

before or after dessert?

Up to you. If you're drinking a fine red with your main course you may want to follow with cheese as the French do, but if you prefer to finish the meal on a savory note, or with a fortified wine like port, save the cheese board until the end of the meal.

Sauvignon Blanc and Appleby's Cheshire

what to drink with ...

soft cheeses

- Whites often go better than reds, particularly with young fresh cheeses.
- **Sauvignon Blanc** with goat cheese and garlic flavored roulés is wonderful.
- Soft fruity reds like **Pinot Noir** and **Merlot** work well with white rinded cheeses like Brie and Camembert and with rich creamy cheeses such as Explorateur.
- **Normandy cider** and Camembert is a great match.

hard cheeses

- Probably the easiest type of cheese to pair with a good red though some alpine cheeses such as Beaufort are equally enjoyable with a very dry white.
- Mature Gouda and cheddar-style cheeses and hard sheep's milk cheeses are the kindest to fine wines like red **Bordeaux** and other top **Cabernets**. Or even a sliver of Parmesan. Milder English regional cheeses such as Cheshire or Caerphilly can be enjoyable with **Sauvignon Blanc**.

strong cheeses

- Any cheese that has been matured to the extent that its flavor and aroma are really pungent is likely to cause problems, whether it's a notoriously strong cheese like Epoisses or a normally mild one like Brie. Aromatic whites such as **Alsace Gewurztraminer** and **Tokay Pinot Gris** are most likely to work as do big reds like **Bordeaux** or **Burgundy**.
- A less conventional but surprisingly successful solution is a Belgian or northern French Trappist-style **beer** such as **Chimay Bleu** or a **Marc de Champagne**.

blue cheeses

- The trickiest cheeses to match, though there are some glorious exceptions such as **Sauternes** and Roquefort.
- In general sweet wines work best with blues, though a full-bodied fruity red such as **Zinfandel** or **Amarone** can be enjoyable in the same way as **Port**. Lesser known **Hungarian Tokaji** is a great wine for blue cheese.
- If you really want to be adventurous try a strong **British vintage ale**.

cooking cheese

Almost any cheese can be used in cooking but some are more suited to it than others. In general harder cheeses melt better, though you can bake softer ones such as goat cheese and Camembert.

melting

Cheddar and cheddar-style cheeses are the most flexible flavorsome cheeses to use for sauces and toppings. Use stronger flavored cheeses rather than milder ones as you will need less, which makes the sauce lighter. Blue cheeses such as **Gorgonzola** can work well in sauces too but use them in moderation as cooking intensifies their flavor. **Mozzarella** is of course the traditional cheese for topping pizza and **Gruyère** and **Emmental** for fondue (see p. 56).

broiling

Small **goat cheeses** (*crottins*) or slices of a goat cheese log broil wonderfully—an easy starter with a few lightly dressed salad leaves.

baking

Soft cheeses such as **Camembert**, **Brie**, and **Vacherin Mont d'Or** can be baked whole in a moderate oven—an instant fondue.

stuffing

Soft cheeses such **Ricotta** can be combined with fresh herbs or greens to stuff a chicken or as a filling for ravioli or canneloni.

grating

Finely grated **Parmigiano-Reggiano** is the perfect cheese for sprinkling over pasta or other cooked dishes. It also combines well with breadcrumbs to make a crusty topping or coating. Or try **Pecorino Romano** and **Ricotta Salata**.

cooking tips

• Unless you're baking a whole cheese, cut the rind off before using cheese in a recipe and cut it into fine slices or grate it so that it melts quickly.

• Cheese is easier to grate or slice straight from the refrigerator but leave it to come to room temperature before adding it to a dish.

• If you're adding it to a sauce, take the sauce off the heat first and add the cheese bit by bit until it has melted. Reheat just enough to melt the cheese. Cheese cooked too long or at too high a temperature will become rubbery and stringy.

frying

Works well with slightly elastic cheeses such as Greek **Halloumi** and **Mozzarella** which makes a delicious fried sandwich (Mozzarella in *carozza*).

If you're making a dish as simple as fondue you need to use top quality cheese. Emmental and Gruyère are traditional but once you've got the hang of it you can play around with other alternatives.

luxury cheese fondue

About 14 oz finely sliced or coarsely grated cheese, with rinds removed: (5 oz Gruyere or Comté, 5 oz Beaufort and 4 oz Emmental, or 8 oz Gruyère and 7 oz Emmental)

2 teaspoons all-purpose flour

1 clove of garlic, halved

¾ cup very dry white wine (e.g. Muscadet)

1 tablespoon kirsch (optional)

Freshly ground nutmeg and black pepper

A cast iron fondue pan and burner

Sourdough, pain de campagne, or ciabatta to serve

Serves 2

Toss the sliced or grated cheese with the flour. Leave until it comes to room temperature.

Rub the inside of the pan with the cut garlic. Start off the fondue on your cooker. Pour in the wine and heat until almost boiling. Remove from the heat and add about a third of the cheese. Keep breaking up the cheese with a wooden spoon using a zig-zag motion as if you were using a wire whisk. (Stirring it round and round as you do with a sauce makes it more likely that the cheese will separate from the liquid).

Once the cheese has begun to melt return it over a very low heat, stirring continuously. Gradually add the remaining cheese until you have a smooth, thick mass (this takes about 10 minutes, less with practice). If it seems too thick add some more hot wine. Add the kirsch, if you like, and season with nutmeg and pepper.

Place over your fondue burner and serve with small bite-size chunks of sourdough or country bread.

Use long fondue forks to dip the bread in, stirring the fondue to prevent it solidifying.

sweet cheese

Accompanied by fruits or drizzled with honey, soft creamy cheeses make a fabulous dessert.

Cheeses that suit the sweet-toothed include fromage frais, Quark, and ultra creamy Mascarpone (even if it doesn't strictly count as cheese). There's a fine dividing line between a cheese plate that serves as a savory and one that replaces a sweet, but if you're looking for the latter you don't want a cheese that's too salty, or fruit that's too tart.

Summer combinations that work well include **strawberries** and **fromage frais, cherries** and **cream cheese** mixed with a little sour cream, and ripe **peaches** and **Mascarpone**. In fall and winter you can serve fruit that has been poached or baked in a fruit syrup, such as **pears** or **prunes** in **red wine** or a **spiced fruit compote**.

Drizzling a cheese with **honey**—even a blue cheese—immediately takes it into the dessert league, particularly if you accompany it with fruit—the classic combination being creamy **Gorgonzola** and **fresh figs**. Soft-set artisanal **jams**, particularly those made from **blueberries** and **plums**, also taste good with rich creamy cheeses. And you can even bake an **apple pie** with cheese, as they do in Yorkshire, England using the local **Wensleydale** cheese.

Mascarpone doubles for cream in all kinds of dishes including the famous Italian tiramisù (it's always a wicked combination with chocolate) and also makes luscious ice cream. My favorite dessert cheese however is **Ricotta** which lends itself perfectly to baking and combines beautifully with **lemon**. It's a thrifty product made from the whey left over from making harder cheeses and gives a lovely light creamy texture to Italian-style cakes and cheesecakes. Make sure you buy the sweet version and not the salty Ricotta Salata.

sweet heaven ...
Mascarpone and **ripe peaches**.

delicious ...
creamy **Gorgonzola** and **fresh figs** drizzled with **honey**.

blueberry cheesecake

This has been my favorite cheesecake recipe since my friend Joan gave me the recipe 20 years ago. I try other recipes but always go back to it.

For the crust:

4 tablespoons unsalted butter

3½ oz graham crackers, crushed into fine crumbs

For the first layer:

2 x 8-oz packages Philadelphia cheese

2 large eggs

½ cup sugar

¼ teaspoon vanilla extract

For the second layer:

1¼ cups sour cream

⅔ cup thick Greek-style yogurt

2½ tablespoons sugar

1 teaspoon vanilla extract

For the topping:

¼ cup caster sugar

8 oz blueberries

1 teaspoon arrowroot

You'll need an 8-in. spring form pan

Serves 8–10

Preheat the oven to 375ºF.

Gently melt the butter in a saucepan, cool slightly and add the crushed biscuits. Press evenly into the base of the cake pan.

Beat the ingredients for the first layer together thoroughly, pour over the biscuit base and smooth the top. Place the pan on a baking sheet and bake in the oven for 20 minutes or until just set. Set aside for 20 minutes to firm up.

Mix the ingredients for the second layer and spoon evenly over the first layer. Return to the oven for 10 minutes then take out and cool.

Refrigerate for at least 6 hours or overnight.

For the topping heat the sugar gently with 2 tablespoons water until it dissolves. Turn up the heat, add the blueberries, cover and cook, shaking the pan occasionally for about 5 minutes until the berries are soft. Take off the heat. Mix the arrowroot with 2 tablespoons water and add to the blueberries. Stir over a gentle heat until the juice has thickened. Set aside to cool. Check for sweetness and add extra sugar to taste.

About an hour before serving ease a knife down the sides of the cake pan then release the clamp and remove the sides. Spoon the blueberry topping evenly over the cheesecake and return to the refrigerator until ready to serve.

You can substitute cranberries for blueberries at Christmas time or simply top with fresh berries.

where to buy great cheese

US

Artisan Cheese
2413 California St.
San Francisco
415 929 8610
www.tomalesbayfoods.com

Artisanal
2 Park Avenue (at 32nd St)
New York 10016
212 725 8585

Murray's Cheeses
257 Bleecker Street
New York 10014
212 243 5001
www.murrayscheese.com

Zingerman's Delicatessen
422 Detroit St
Ann Arbor
MI 48104
734 663 3354
www.zingermans.com

UK & IRELAND

The Fine Cheese Company
29 & 31 Walcot Street
Bath BA1 5BN
+44 (0)1225 448748
www.finecheese.co.uk

La Fromagerie
2–4 Moxon Street
London W1U 4EW
+44 (0)20 7935 0341
www.lafromagerie.co.uk

Iain Mellis Cheesemonger
30a Victoria Street
Edinburgh EH1 2JW
+44 (0)131 226 6215

Neal's Yard Dairy
17 Shorts Gardens
Covent Garden
London WC2H 9AT
+44 (0)20 7645 3553
mailorder@nealsyarddairy.co.uk

and
Borough Market
6 Park Street
London SE1 9AB
+44 (0)20 7645 3554

Paxton and Whitfield
93 Jermyn Street
London SW1Y 6JE
Mail order: +44 (0)1608 652090
www.cheesemongers.co.uk

Sheridan's Cheesemongers
11 South Anne Street
Dublin 2
+353 (01) 679 3143
Online only:
www.thecheesesociety.co.uk

FRANCE

Androuet
Three branches in Paris including
rue Arsène-Houssaye
Paris 8e
01 42 89 95 00

Marie-Anne Cantin
12 rue du Champ-de-Mars
Paris 7e
01 45 50 43 94
www.cantin.fr

Philippe Olivier
43 rue Thiers
62200 Boulogne-sur-Mer
03 21 31 94 74
www.philippe-olivier.com

Online only: www.fromages.com

AUSTRALIA

GPO Cheese Room
No. 1 Martin Place
Sydney
NSW 2000
02 9229 7704

Richmond Hill Cafe and Larder
40–50 Bridge Road
Richmond
Melbourne
03 1 9421 2808
www.rhcl.com.au

OTHER GOOD CHEESE WEBSITES

www.ilovecheese.com
Very user-friendly website hosted
by the American Dairy
Association, with recipes from
leading US chefs, food and wine
pairing suggestions and home
tasting "kits".

www.cheese.com
Encyclopaedic index of 652
cheeses, classified by name,
country, texture and milk.

www.thecheeseweb.com
Cheese expert Juliet Harbutt's
website. Carries information
about the British Cheese Awards.

**www.specialistcheesemakers.
co.uk**
Website of the Specialist
Cheesemakers Association. Lists
British cheeses with links to
producers.

www.cheesemaking.org
Website of the American Cheese
Society. Lists American cheeses
and cheesemakers.

www.slowfood.it
Comprehensive section on Italian
cheeses.

Recommended reading
Cheese by Juliet Harbutt (1999
Mitchell Beazley, London)
The Cheese Plate by Max
McCalman and David Gibbons,
(2002 Clarkson Potter, New York)
Steven Jenkins Cheese Primer
(1996 Workman, New York)
The Cheese Room by Patricia
Michelson (2001 Michael Joseph,
London)

index

conversion charts

Weights and measures have been rounded up or down slightly to make measuring easier.

Volume equivalents:

American	Metric	Imperial
1 teaspoon	5 ml	
1 tablespoon	15 ml	
¼ cup	60 ml	2 fl.oz.
⅓ cup	75 ml	2½ fl.oz.
½ cup	125 ml	4 fl.oz.
⅔ cup	150 ml	5 fl.oz. (¼ pint)
¾ cup	175 ml	6 fl.oz.
1 cup	250 ml	8 fl.oz.

Weight equivalents: **Measurements:**

Imperial	Metric	Inches	Cm
1 oz.	25 g	¼ inch	5 mm
2 oz.	50 g	½ inch	1 cm
3 oz.	75 g	¾ inch	1.5 cm
4 oz.	125 g	1 inch	2.5 cm
5 oz.	150 g	2 inches	5 cm
6 oz.	175 g	3 inches	7 cm
7 oz.	200 g	4 inches	10 cm
8 oz. (½ lb.)	250 g	5 inches	12 cm
9 oz.	275 g	6 inches	15 cm
10 oz.	300 g	7 inches	18 cm
11 oz.	325 g	8 inches	20 cm
12 oz.	375 g	9 inches	23 cm
13 oz.	400 g	10 inches	25 cm
14 oz.	425 g	11 inches	28 cm
15 oz.	475 g	12 inches	30 cm
16 oz. (1 lb.)	500 g		
2 lb.	1 kg		

Oven temperatures:

110°C	(225°F)	Gas ¼
120°C	(250°F)	Gas ½
140°C	(275°F)	Gas 1
150°C	(300°F)	Gas 2
160°C	(325°F)	Gas 3
180°C	(350°F)	Gas 4
190°C	(375°F)	Gas 5
200°C	(400°F)	Gas 6
220°C	(425°F)	Gas 7
230°C	(450°F)	Gas 8
240°C	(475°F)	Gas 9